# THE STAUFFERS

# Jussi Salemaa

# The Stauffers

## Their Roots and Settling in Finland in the 1800s

Stauffer family

Helsinki 2025

Original Finnish Edition: Jussi Salemaa, Stauffer-suvun juuret ja kotiu-
tuminen Suomeen 1800-luvulla, 1985.

© 1985, 2025 The Estate of Jussi Salemaa

Layout and cover: Jaakko Salemaa

Publisher: BoD · Books on Demand, Mannerheimintie 12 B,

00100 Helsinki, bod@bod.fi

Print: Libri Plureos GmbH, Friedensallee 273, 22763 Hampuri, Saksa

ISBN 978-952-80-9496-8

## PREFACE TO THE FINNISH EDITION

In the great hunger years of the 1860s three Stauffer brothers from Simmental in Switzerland arrived in Elimäki to work as cattle breeders and dairymen on the af Forselleses' estates. These young men became attached to the soil of this chilly country and later achieved the position of independent estate owner and cheese trader. Some decades later three of their sisters together with husbands and children followed in their footsteps. The brothers and their brothers-in-law played a significant role in introducing and consolidating cheese dairying in Finland.

This has been a vigorous family. Today when the fifth and sixth generations in Finland are assuming responsibility for the continuity of life, the number of living members of the family is approaching four hundred.

When planning the Stauffers' family get-together that was held in Elimäki on the 6th of July, the undersigned was given the task of drawing up an account of the family's background and early events in Finland. At the request of the family, and with some addenda and photographs, this will be published in booklet form and distributed to members of the family.

I would like to thank the family members for the information and photographs I have received. Seppo Soratie, who has done a great job of clarifying the course of Samuel Stauffer's life and outlining the branches of the family that remained in Switzerland, deserves particular thanks. In this he has been given valuable help by our second cousin, Adolf Zwalen-Nobs.

This booklet has been printed with a subsidy from Sirkka Paatela.

Helsinki, September 1985

Jussi Salemaa

## NOTE TO THE ENGLISH EDITION

My father Jussi Salemaa translated his historical essay on the Stauffer family into English so that the relatives in Switzerland to whom he sent copies could read it too. One of the immigrant Sttauffer brothers was his grandfather Jakob.

Nearly 40 years after the booklet came out in Finnish, it is now published in English. Mike Vollar kindly checked the language and modernized spelling.

Helsinki, February 2025

Jaakko Salemaa

# Leaving Simmental in Switzerland

It is the summer of 1864 at Samuel Stauffer's mountain farm in Ringoldingen, Simmental. The sturdy farmhouse is crowded. Samuel's extensive family is sitting together at table and finishing their "rösti" supper. At one end sits the head of the household thoughtfully scrutinising his wife Katharina, Bütschi's daughter from lower down the Simme, who is sitting opposite him.

Seated on one side of the table are the daughters Katharina (32), Anna (30), Magdalena (27), Elisabeth (22), Verena (19), Susanna (16), and Rosina (13). On the other side are the sons Samuel (29), Johann (26), Christian (25), Peter (21), and Jakob (18). In the background stand daughter-in-law Magdalena, married to Samuel, the eldest daughter's husband Christian Teuscher, and the school-teacher Friedrich Wiedmer, Anna's fiancé.

Samuel the elder is looking at his sons, who are getting ready to leave.

| | |
|---|---|
| Samuel | Don't leave yet, boys. I have something to tell you. This "rösti" of ours was delicious, but talking of potatoes I suppose you have noticed the potato blight in our neighbour's field. That means tomorrow it will be here. Where has that pest come from again? |
| Samuel Jr. | It's carried on the wind from Wallis. The French always suffer from it there. It was the strong wind in March that brought it here. |
| Samuel | It doesn't come with the wind. But I don't want to argue about that matter now, I've got something else on my mind. I was in Erlenbach this morning and saw the vicar. He told me he had received a letter from Finland. |

| | |
|---|---|
| Katharina | What's he talking to you about his letters for? And what is this Finland? |
| Wiedmer | I know. It belongs to Russia, a sort of Grand Duchy. They are ruled by the same prince as the Russians. It is north of the capital, Saint Petersburg. |
| Samuel | The vicar told me that a noble gentleman by the name of af Forselles and his relatives will begin cheese production on their estates in Elimäki in Finland. There are already a few Swiss there but they need half a dozen more young men who know how to make cheese. They are the owners of large estates, thousands of acres of fields and meadows, as much as in the whole of Simmental. The vicar was asking whether our Christian and Peter could go there since they don't have much work. He has money and instructions for the journey. |
| Katharina | Bless me, don't talk about things like that, they are just children. You needn't take the blight as seriously as that. We've had it before, haven't we, and we have a lot of cheese in our cellar and some money too. I hear they are beginning to build an artillery barracks in Thun, and there will always be some work at the hotels in Interlaken. Isn't Finland further away than America? |
| Samuel | You surely know what it will mean for us if we need to buy potatoes. Food grain needs to be bought anyway. Don't you remember ten years ago when frost often caught the crops and potatoes were damaged by blight? One had to give a centner of cheese for one hectolitre of grain. And besides, as a Simmental woman I'm sure you are aware what life is like in this valley. Our sons are not the first who will leave this wretched place. There is talk of a worldwide depression again. I don't know precisely what it means, but for us it will mean a fall in the price of cheese. |

| | |
|---|---|
| Christian | I know that business of the Forselleses. Yesterday I called in at the Klossners', and the aunt had received a letter from her son Rudolf. He has already been in Finland for about ten years, making cheese at the Sippola estate for von Daehn. Rudolf says in his letter that he has been talking to these Forselleses, and that they have been keeping an eye on Daehn's undertakings for a long time and decided to follow his lead and intensify their cattle rearing. They have even asked Rudolf to search for competent men to come to Finland. Otherwise Rudolf says that the country is good, although winter is very severe. The country folk are like people here, very industrious in growing food grain, but they don't understand stock breeding. Cows are kept only for manure for the fields, and in winter they are fed straw and twigs. They are closed up indoors for most of the year. |
| Samuel | Rudolf's written then? I met this Daehn while he was here, it must have been in 1856 when he took Rudolf on. He was driving a two-horse team and we bumped into each other at the bridge when I was carrying a load of cheese to Erlenbach. He was a very inquisitive man, asking all sorts of things about our farming. He asked for a bit of cheese, praised its taste, and said that one could get a high price for it on the St Petersburg market. |
| | He gave me a silver coin with a double-headed eagle on it, and I got 50 rappens for it at a jeweller's in Thun. Maybe he is a rich man. Anyway the fact is that there are too many of us around this table. |
| Anna | I won't be sitting at this table long. Friedrich has got a teaching job in Murten and we will be moving there soon. |
| Peter | The case is as father said. To mother I'd like to say that Thun people have their own unemployed folk to maintain, so they won't employ us. And as for Interlaken, |

carrying Englishmen's suitcases and bowing to them with hand outstretched isn't fit work for a man. There would be work in the factories in Zurich, but I don't want to go there. It's miserable to slave in a factory when one is used to a different kind of work.

Jakob    What about enrolling in some German prince's army?

Samuel    Forget it. Soldiers are no longer needed. There will be no wars any longer. You've read about the Holy Alliance, haven't you? An eternal peace is prevailing now. And on the other hand a soldier's life isn't much good. Remember that in this valley there are still some invalids crippled during Napoleon's Moscow campaign living here on charity.

Jakob    Yes, it's no good living here. Peace might be eternal, but even here there is the never-ending spreading of manure on meadows. You'd think that grass would grow even without all that manuring.

Samuel    No it wouldn't, son. We wouldn't be able to keep six cows on this patch if the meadows didn't get plenty of manure.

The vicar told me that the salary Forselles are offering is good. I have calculated that living economically you could have enough saved up in 30 years that you could come back here, buy a house in Spiez, and live there on your savings. Then you could help me keep up my farm sometimes.

Katharina    Poor Samuel, you won't be around any more by then. You can be certain that if the boys go away you will never see them again. What did you say to the vicar?

Samuel    I said that Christian and Peter will go. It's a bit of luck that you will go to Finland to earn money because I've got something else to tell you. I'm an old man and I often feel pain under my breastbone. I'm no longer able to run this farm. I have thought about things and talked to mother about transferring this farm to young Samuel to be redeemed, him being the eldest son.

I have found a smaller farm on the slope of Rinderberg, you know, that mountain above Zweisimmen. The house is in a beautiful place, rather high up. There I'll be able to breathe more easily than here at the bottom of this misty valley.

So we'll be moving there with Johann and the girls. Jakob can stay here if he likes to help Samuel, or come with us to Zweisimmen.

| | |
|---|---|
| Christian | That's settled then. Peter and I will be leaving for Finland although I think that father farming with Johann's help won't be much of a success. I know my brother, he's too keen on yodelling and forgets his work. How do we get to Elimäki? |
| Johann | When you have got a house in Finland I'll come and yodel to your heart's content. |
| Samuel | Be quiet now. The vicar will explain the route in more detail and give you the passports and money for the journey. You go first to Thun and from there to Basel by train. There is a train carriage leaving once a week direct to Saint Petersburg, where the af Forselleses have living quarters. They will arrange a horse-coach for you to Elimäki. The vicar estimates that you will be there in a week if everything goes well. |
| Katharina | It's not so far away then. America would be further away, wouldn't it? I hope you don't fall out of the train. |
| Samuel | I'll give you money for the return journey in case living there proves too difficult, which I don't actually believe. Mother has woven half a dozen new cheese cloths that you can take with you to get properly started. I imagine |

|                |                                                                                          |
| -------------- | ---------------------------------------------------------------------------------------- |
|                | there is so much woodland in Finland that you'll be able to have mould boards made. Then you can make your cheese assuming you have the patience to keep the vat and pails clean. Educated people claim that there are bacteria which live in the dirt. |
| Susanna        | That's not true. My teacher said that bacteria just turn milk into cheese. |
| Samuel         | Be that as it may, you'll end up with something useless if you don't keep the pails clean. And don't come back immediately. Try to find and marry good frugal wives, farmers' daughters, who can help you and teach you the local language. No-one can understand this schwyz-erdytsch of ours, as I found out when having that talk with Daehn. |
| Jakob          | I'm not going either to Finland or to Zweisimmen, I'm going to France with Zenger's son. There was a "Seelen-verkaüfer" (immigration official) here and he promised work at a meat processing plant near Paris. |
| Katharina      | I can't get it into my head that the boys have to leave. But when the time comes I'll put a lump of sugar dipped in "Kirsch" into your mouth so that I know you'll be back again soon. |

This fragment of fictional conversation demonstrates quite a number of the background factors behind the departure of the Stauffer brothers as well as about ten other young men from Simmental to Finland in the 1860s and 1870s. The severity of living conditions in their home valley as well as encouragement from Rudolf Klossner, who had emigrated to the Sippola estate in Finland from a neighbouring village, were the factors responsible for setting them on their way to this unfamiliar corner of the north. Katharina's hope that she would get her sons back again wasn't realised. Before her death she was to see two of her daughters' families leaving for Finland too.

Katharina, mother of Stauffer brothers and
sisters, born Bütschi (1810–1894).

# The Facts behind the Story above

Christian and Peter left for Elimäki in Finland in 1864, Christian to the Moisio estate owned by Colonel Teodor Ulrik af Forselles and Peter to the Myllylä estate owned by young Oskar af Forselles. Jakob went to Paris but was dissatisfied with the conditions there and soon came back to the home valley. He was about to leave for America when it was agreed within the family that he would go to Finland in place of Christian, who was to come back home to help his father out. Jakob followed in his brothers' footsteps to Finland in the spring of 1867, a spring that was extremely cold and brought on the last and the most destructive year of famine in Finland. At first he entered the service of Moisio's colonel as planned, but after Christian's return to Moisio in 1874 he moved to Per Emil af Forselles' neighbouring Peippola estate.

Samuel the elder also stuck to his plan and left Ringoldingen. In the same autumn that Christian and Peter went to Finland he moved to the Zweisimmen region 20 kms up the Simme. His new farm was in the village of Weiermatt about two kilometres south of Zweisimmen on the slope of Rinderberg. The farmhouse from Samuel's time is still in use. Its position at an altitude of 1500 m was good only for mountain farming, i.e. cattle breeding and cheese making.

This is where Samuel spent the rest of his life. Christian's prediction about his father farming with Johann's help turned out to be true, so he had to come back from Finland and help his father for five years. The reason for Christian returning may have been that they didn't want to allow the young Jakob to go as far away as America and thus he was given the possibility to find work nearer the home country.

Samuel died in 1881 at the age of 80. After her husband's death Katharina moved back to the region of Erlenbach, where she died in 1894 at the age of 84, living her final years with daughter Magdalena and family.

Samuel Stauffer had been born in the village of Diessbach in 1801, some ten kilometres from Thun towards Bern. The events of his early years are unknown but it can be supposed that he was still quite young when he found himself in the Simme valley, where he met his wife-to-be Katharina Bütschi from Reutigen at the mouth of the Simme. The wedding took place in 1831 when Samuel was 30 and Katharina 10 years younger. The birth-places of the children allow us to trace the family's movements. The elder Samuel, apparently working as a herdsman or tenant farmer, was wandering around the Nieder-Simmental villages (one of which was Diemtigen) with his rapidly growing family until 1847. This was when he acquired the farm in the village of Ringoldingen in Erlenbach parish, the village where Samuel's sons and daughters spent their childhood and youth.

Samuel's and Katharina's daughters got married: Anna to Friedrich Wiedmer, Verena to Benedickt Weibel and Susanna to Christian Eggen. Wiedmer and Eggen came from Simmental and Weibel from Rapperswill near Bern. At the brothers' suggestion they emigrated to Finland with their families, the Wiedmers and the Weibels in the 1880s and the Eggens in the 1890s.

Thus six of Samuel's and Katharina's 12 children had found a new home country and quickly and firmly became rooted in the soil of Finland. Only Susanna's and her husband's stay in Finland remained short.

Katharina was related to the Kernen and the Fuhrer families, and men from both of these also emigrated to Finland. It is quite possible that Edvard Bütschi who emigrated from Reutigen to Finland in 1908 was a grandson of Katharina's brother.

# Relatives in Switzerland

Of Samuel's and Katharina's children who remained in Switzerland, their eldest son Samuel is worth mentioning; at first he continued cattle breeding and cheese making with his father in Weiermatt and later in Garstatt, 4 km north of Zweisimmen, on the mountain farm which he bought. According to his daughter Rosa Zwalen both her father and grandfather – Samuel the elder – were the most talented of the cattle breeders in the valley. They leased extensive pastures on the slopes of Rinderberg and Kaltenbrunn where their many head of cattle were brought up to within reach of the snowline in spring. Cheese was made in Alpine huts (Sennerei) and whey was cooked into sugar. In autumn the cattle were brought down in stages to Weiermatt and then further down the valley to be tended in cowsheds. The Fürsteini farm in Garstatt is still owned by the family. Rosa told how Katharina, her grandmother on her father's side, was a very alert and active old lady who still managed to do needle-work without wearing glasses when she was over 80 years old. She wrote short letters to her children in Finland, of which a few have been preserved.

The cramped home valley wasn't capable of providing a livelihood for the younger Samuel's children either. All his three sons spent their adult years running leased dairies on estates in Livonia.

The second son Johann died childless. In 1898 he visited his brothers and sisters in Finland where, inspired by the rugged scenery of the Miettilä ridge in Rautu, he kept his promise of entertaining Christian's family with his yodelling.

The daughters Katharina, Magdalena and Elisabeth married mountain farmers from their home valley. Elisabeth's son Jakob Bühler came to Finland as a youngster in the early 1900s and died at the age of 20 at the Weibels' place in Heinjoki in 1905.

Nothing is known about the life of the youngest daughter, Rosina.

Some branches of the family in Switzerland have proliferated considerably. The younger generations of the Finnish branch of the family are known to have about a hundred fourth- and fifth-generation cousins in Switzerland.

Most of the family members didn´t stay in the home valley. Many have settled down in the Lausanne, Basel and Zürich regions while at the same time the family's professional profile has changed radically. Mountain farmers are few and far between. But in the home valley there are still a number of family members carrying on the ancestral profession with surnames such as Teuscher, Imobersteg and Siegenthaler.

The male branch of the family has died out in the Simme valley. The childhood home in Ringoldingen has been demolished but it is known to have been situated lower down in the valley near the riverside.

# The Simmental Area – Its Geographical, Historical and Agricultural Features

The Simme, in whose valley the Stauffer brothers and sisters were born and spent their youth, is not a great river. At the tiny village of Ringoldingen the width of the river-bed is about ten metres. In spring and summer snow and ice are melting in the Alps and the stream has a torrential flow of water. In winter it runs dry. The Simme rises in the Berner Oberland mountain range and flows first north, before turning east at Boltimgen towards Lake Thun into which it empties between Spiez and Thun, two towns famed for their beauty.

The most notable village along the 10 km-long Nieder-Simmental is Erlenbach. Ringoldingen is situated 2 km to the west of this and Diemtigen, the home village of Rudolf Klossner and many other cheesemakers who emigrated to Finland, 1½ km to the south-east on the slopes of a tributary valley. The population of Erlenbach parish in the middle of the 19th century was approximately one thousand. Half lived in the beautifully built traditional Swiss-style church village, while the other half was spread throughout half a dozen hamlets and scattered settlements. Ringoldingen consisted of 20-30 households.

It is 20 km from Erlenbach to the nearest town of any size, Thun, and 25 km more to Bern, the capital of the canton and of the whole country.

The valley of the Simme is narrow and steep-sloped. The shore of the winding river-bed is bordered by a flat strip of land only a couple of hundred metres wide. Ringoldingen is 700 m above sea-level. The terrain begins to rise steeply so that at a distance of 1 km from the river the altitude is already 1000 m and soon the mountains on both sides of the river have summits at over 2000 m above sea-level in places. Niesen to the south stands at 2360 m and Stockhorn to the north at 2160 m.

The climate of the region doesn't differ substantially from weather conditions in southern Finland. Down in the valley the mean annual temperature is +7° (Elimäki +4°), for July +16° (Elimäki +15°), and for January -2° (Elimäki -8°). In Ringoldingen apple trees are already in blossom in April. Higher up on the slopes at 1000–1500 m, for example in Weiermatt, the temperature statistics correspond more or less to those in Elimäki, the main difference being in annual rainfall. This is over 1000 mm, or twice the rainfall in Finland. Fog, mist and haze often lie over the valley.

Nieder-Simmental and Erlenbach are visible on the map to the west of Lake Thun. Tourist map: Karl Baedeker, *Die Schweiz, Handbuch für Reisende*, Leipzig 1913.

The Berner Oberland valleys were already populated during the Bronze Age between 1800–800 B.C. There was a bronze foundry in Wimmis at the mouth of the Simme.

Migration of Celtic and Helvetic tribes to the region began in 400 B.C. and ended around the time of Christ's birth when the Romans occupied the land. Erlenbach (in Latin Chlusi, a guard-post) and Zweisimmen (Romestalde) were established during Roman times. Roman rule came to an end in about 450 A.D. when a Germanic tribe the Alemannes conquered the northern areas of Switzerland which nowadays constitute its German-speaking area. Place names ending in -igen, -ingen and -will such as Ringoldingen and Diemtigen derive from Alemannic. The family name Stauffer derives from the word "Stauf", a bowl or beaker. So one of the family's distant ancestors might well have been a bowl-maker by profession. There are a number of places and mountains in Switzerland and southern Germany whose names are based on the word "Stauf" such as Staufen and Staufberg. Here the name probably refers to the bowl-type shape of the terrain. The Stauffer surname is not unknown in and around Bern where there are several dozen of them.

Along the course of the Simme runs a main road built during Roman times linking the valley to Thun, and the Thun-Spiez-Montreux railway line, the Spiez-Erlenbach part of which was completed in 1897, i.e. after the youngsters had left.

The inhabitants, comprising for the main part in the 1860s (as still today) small independent family farms based on cattle breeding, are concentrated around the river and the road on the slopes facing south. There are only a few farms on the higher slopes. In the 1800s mountain farmers in Simmental cultivated a certain amount of animal feed and root crops, with perhaps a little grain for human consumption in the most favourable places. Nowadays this has been discontinued with only meadowland remaining.

Guide-books tend to praise the scenery around Simmental as picturesque. It's easy enough to share this opinion as long as we keep in mind that it is wild and barren and typified by bare grey cliffs and dense forests of spruce. In Ringoldingen down in the lower valley the views by no means always open out into sweeping Alpine vistas. In misty weather when visibility is poor, the green meadows on the slopes and the dark belts of spruce which intersect them produce an effect which would not be out of place in a Finnish hilly landscape. We are not likely to be far wrong if we envisage Christian and Jakob in their latter days on the highish hills of southern Rautu and on the spruce-lined banks of the Kymi river, recalling a sense of their childhood landscapes.

Erlenbach im Simmental, the home municipality of Stauffer family. Ringoldingen is located 2 km west (to the left) from the church at the centre of the picture. Postcard probably from 1920s.

One of the most popular tourist routes in the 19th century between Thun and Interlaken skirted the estuary of the Simme. Interlaken's development into a flourishing centre of tourism must also have had an effect on the life of people in Simmental. The valley itself with its lack of attractive sights must have remained pure "Hirtenland". Which it still is, particularly as regards the Nieder-Simmental, though even here

20

touring and recreational skiing bring business and colour to the life of the locals. There are several hotels in Erlenbach and a cableway to Stockhorn. Even Ringoldingen now has its own little hotel-restaurant "Jäger". The actual focal points for tourism and winter sports are situated on the upper course and headwaters of the Simme.

The forests in this area are mostly protected woodland which cannot be felled, so that their significance for the local economy commercially speaking has remained slight. It is known that in the 19th century mountain farmers in Ringoldingen got timber for their household use from their own spinnies.

There was no industrial activity in the valley. Subcontracting work for the watch industry, which in the 19th century flourished in the mountain villages of French-speaking cantons, didn't gain a foothold on the Berner Oberland side.

Cattle breeding was the main source of livelihood in Simmental. Mountain dwellers must have had to concentrate all their labour and energy on this and on refining its products, which by the 1850s was already highly intensive. As a result of hundreds of years of selective breeding they had succeeded in developing a high milk-producing Simmental breed with an annual yield of 2000 litres using domestic fodder. Particular attention was paid to upkeep of the pasture and keeping it fertilised.

From an economic point of view the most valuable product developed was a type of cheese intended originally for domestic and local consumption which, on account of its taste and above all its good storage and transport properties, was starting to gain extensive markets abroad.

Milk was made into cheese in 400–500 litre cauldrons over an open fire. According to need the heat for the cauldron could be turned up or down by means of a trammel hook. The product would then be called a mini- or pre-emmental. The wheel weighed only 30–40 kilos and somewhat resembled a modern-day gruyère. In the latter half of the 19th century, by enlarging the size of the cauldron and fine-tuning the production method, this was developed into an 80–100 kilo cheese wheel with large holes which was granted the brand-name *Emmental*.

Originally cheese was only made during summertime on the Alpine pastures, but even in the 18th century its production was spreading to the mountain villages and from there, at the beginning of the 19th century, to Switzerland's more agricultural regions. At the same time production was increasing and it became an export commodity of immense importance.

Cheesemaking at a Swiss alpine dairy ("Sennerei") in the 18th century. Copper engraving: J.J. Scheuchzer, *Naturgeschichten des Schweizerlandes*, Zürich 1707. National Library of Finland.

It can be mentioned that annual Swiss cheese production in 1810 amounted to one million kilos, of which half was exported. By 1880 the respective amounts were 20 million and 10 million kilos. At that time there were 2500 cheese producers (Sennerei) in the country and 3000 village dairy co-operatives. Production of butter even then was so alien that it needed to be imported. Care was taken to avoid over-production of cheese and so the problem arising from the increase in milk production was solved by establishing Europe's first factory for condensing milk in 1867 and in finding profitable uses for it.

In Finland production of one million kilos was attained in the early 1900s and 20 million kilos only in 1952. As in Switzerland, half of this was exported.

Samuel the elder is known to have run a village dairy in Ringoldingen. How large his cheese production was is not known. Although a larger than normal portion of the milk from the local farms had to be used for feeding pedigree calves being raised for market, we can easily imagine that from the village's twenty or so farms enough milk was accumulated at least during the summer months for producing a 30–40 kilo loaf of cheese most days of the week.

In Switzerland in the 1860s there was as yet no professional schooling in cheese production. Thus the brothers in Finland had to rely on the knowledge and skill they had acquired helping their father with the dairy. At quite an early age the boys had to learn to work independently raising cattle and making cheese during the grazing season when cows and goats were out on the Alpine pastures. It was the practice for the younger generation to stay up in the Alpine huts and take care of the herding and other work associated with dairying.

In the early 19th century the Swiss mountain valleys, where every acre fit for cultivation and pasture had been made use of long ago, and where land fragmentation had already been pushed to its limit, could no longer provide a livelihood and work for the population which was rapidly expanding due to the high birth-rate. The pressure caused by this over-population was mitigated partly by migration to the industrial centres of the homeland and partly in emigration to neighbouring countries, at first mostly to France. This was particularly evident in the mountain-farmer community of Berner Oberland, who preferred emigrating to working in factories. The exodus was intensified owing to the crop failures which were unusually severe in the period 1845–1855. In 1854 emigration, which during this period was mainly towards North America, reached record levels. In this particular year 18 000 people departed their homeland, representing 0.7% of the country's population of 2.6 million. Statistics show that 50 000 Swiss were living abroad as immigrants in 1850, in 1880 250 000 and in 1890 300 000, of whom 140 000 in North America, 80 000 in France, 40 000 in Germany and 2000 in Russia. The number who moved to Finland was in the region of 50 families in 1890.

It was therefore natural and understandable that in the mid-nineteenth century several of the Stauffer family's younger generation were swept up by these burgeoning currents and emigrated. Their departure from Simmental was both forced and straightforward. They didn't have much choice, the only question being when to leave and where to head to. On the other hand the fact that by a stroke of luck they found themselves caught up in a movement outside of the primary emigration streams, namely to Finland, is a matter of interest. 120 years after the event it is difficult to find any other explanation than it being a turn of the wheel of fortune. Christian and Peter happened to be ready and waiting in the right place at the right time, meaning that they already possessed the professional skills needed and a willingness to emigrate. The right place means the neighbourhood of Rudolf Klossner's home and the right moment means when the af Forselleses were contemplating rationalisation of their cattle and dairy business.

In this connection another interesting question emerges. What impulse was behind von Daehn travelling specifically to the Simmental valley in order to employ a cheesemaker for his Sippola estate? On his way deep into the Berner Oberland he would have had to pass through the country's better-known agricultural districts where cheese production was already well established in 1856. For example he had passed by the Emme valley where he could easily have found plenty of young men ready to go to Finland. Could the reason have been that as a keen cattle breeder of pedigree stock von Daehn wanted to get first-hand knowledge of the Simmental breed in its own natural environment? It is tantalising to conjecture that it was only in Diemtigen that he realised the local breed was poorly suited to Finnish conditions, but while learning about the local milk processing decided to begin cheese making on his Sippola farm and hired Klossner to direct it. This decision of his had far-reaching consequences.

One consequence was that from the very beginning cheese production in Finland was concentrated on Emmental-type cheeses. This tendency still prevails and from the point of view of the export market is probably the most economical. It is likely that without von Daehn and the direction taken by him industrial cheese production would have followed a similar development to that in Scandinavian countries and settled for a different kind of product.

Once they had settled down in Finland, as far as is known the brothers never greatly missed the valley of their birth and it is not known that they ever seriously considered resettling in their native country, even though this would have been financially possible much earlier than their father Samuel had envisaged. They did visit Simmental a few times to see their parents and later their mother after the father had died. But on their return to Finland from these trips they used to point out how the atmosphere in the valley was oppressive and living there like "crawling round the bottom of a milk churn".

In their latter days the brothers recalled their youth in Simmental as a tough and frugal time. This is not difficult to understand. In those days farming work which was in any case hard was made even more so in Ringoldingen by the steepness of the terrain. Work on the hillside meadows required sheer physical strength using primitive equipment without draught animals. It was standard practice to mow the home meadows twice during the summer before letting cattle and goats graze on it with the advent of autumn. Continuous mowing on the steep meadow slopes, carrying bundles of hay on their shoulders down into the valley or for haystacks – what was called "höwbärge" in Simmental dialect – to await transportation in the winter, and then lugging manure uphill, were all repetitive and exhausting work. Likewise collecting wood in the winter and transporting it in deep snow on the forest slopes was difficult and tiring. It's not difficult to imagine that dairy farming and production of cheese were a refreshing relief from their traditional way of life.

Simmentalers have earned a reputation for conservatism. Berners say that progress there has taken place despite the resistance of the inhabitants.

There was a strong belief in the valley right into the 19th century that all disasters such as illnesses, crop failures, and animal and plant diseases were carried on the warm south wind, the "Phön" wind. The worst scourge was the flooding of the Simme, which was actually caused by this warm south wind and which in the worst case washed away both top-soil and crops from the fields by the riverbank. In Ringoldingen the terrain was safe inasmuch as snow and avalanches didn't directly threaten village life. Yet herding and mowing on the edges of the slopes was perilous work. While herding goats as a boy Jakob took a wrong step and got into a slide down the steep slope towards a deep gorge. He was saved by grabbing hold of a willow root. In his old days he used to reminisce on this event and while patting a bunch of willow twigs say that a willow had once saved his life.

Emigration before the First World War both from Finland and Switzerland was fairly similar in both quantity and direction. The difference was that in Switzerland it began some 20 years earlier, and climaxed in the crop failures of the 1850s, whereas in Finland it fell round the turn of the century. In any case the similarity in the extent of emigration and its structure indicates that the problems experienced in the Bern Oberland and Finland, with an economy that was still almost exclusively agricultural, were not very different.

The Swiss authorities didn't look on this extensive emigration favourably. It was difficult for them to admit that the reason for the emigration was a poorly administered employment policy, particularly when there would have been sufficient work available in the industrial regions of the country. Instead they began to concoct a theory together with psychologists that a larger than usual love of adventure and a longing to see foreign countries and peoples was instinctive in the Helvetian peoples' basic character. The later direction of waves of emigration has shown this view to be unfounded. By virtue of the *Homestead Act*, which was enacted in the USA in 1862, every male immigrant was entitled free of charge to a land grant of 65 hectares for cultivation, and this was a sufficient inducement for sons of smallholders suffering from land hunger who were unwilling to submit to factory work.

In 1984 a treatise was published by Bern University on the emigration of Berner Oberland cheesemakers to Russia in the 19th century (Paul-Anton Nielson: *"Ein Bruder von dem zu haben", Katalog einer Austellung in der Schweizerischen Landesbibliothek 1984*). The most interesting part of this study concerns an explanation of how emigration to Russia got started and why Diemtigen became the most significant point of departure.

During Napoleon's military campaigns Captain Jakob Mani (1758–1819), the head of the Styg farm in Diemtigen, and Prince Ivan Sergeyevich Meshchersky (1775–1851) from Tver Governorate happened to meet. Under circumstances that remain rather vague, Mani had to promise his master cheesemaker Johannes Müller (1785–1852) to Ivan. At his master's bidding Johannes set out for Tver in 1814. He spent 25 years in Russia and during that time recruited ten of his relatives from Diemtigen and elsewhere in Simmental. He returned to his native area in 1839 so that it is likely that both Rudolf Klossner and Samuel Stauffer would have met this first immigrant to Russia and heard about his experiences there.

The study mentioned above pointed out that in the early 1850s a couple of dozen men from Berner Oberland were working in Russia on cheese production. During the decades to follow the stream of immigration intensified, bringing hundreds of Swiss dairymen to Russian estates, from Livonia to Siberia. Interestingly, the study also points out that recruitment of additional labour from the old homeland required by expanding production of cheese was undertaken preferably from the ranks of one's own family or relatives. Relying on relatives during the early decades of cheese production was a conspicuous feature in Finland too. The Stauffer brothers and their brothers-in-law are a good though far from unique example of this.

Other Simmental men who left for Finland during the early phase of emigration include such names as Bühler, Fuhrer, Kernen, Knutti, Kunz, Marti, Ruchti, Stucki, Treuthardt and Zenger. They had had to live out their youth in their home valley far away from the mainstream of cultural and economic life. With only a few exceptions they had no higher learning but from the perspective of their time they were relatively enlightened and had good reading, writing and arithmetic skills. They were used to hard work and had mastered their professions as cattle breeders and cheesemakers. Naturally in those days they could not have had any theoretical knowledge of the biochemistry pertaining to cheese production nor any possibility for influencing it. Their expertise was built on practical experience.

In the 1870s the source area from which emigrants to Finland were culled was expanded to include other mountain villages in Berner Oberland and across Lake Thun to the valley of the Emme, where Liechti, the Oesches and the Pfäfflis with their relatives came from. In general the Bern canton was and remained during the whole period of emigration until the early 1920s one of the more important source areas.

But this is not to deny that people came from other cantons too. One such was Johann Baumgartner from Sankt Gallen canton who as early as 1858 came to Finland and set up cheese production in Peippola in 1862. Likewise Melchior Britschgi, the cheesemaker for Malmgård estate, was from Ragaz in eastern Switzerland, part of the Retoroman district. Robert Brück, with whom the Stauffer brothers co-operated, was from Gadmen in the east of the country.

Cheesemakers from the French- and Italian-speaking cantons were not attracted to Finland.

# Estate Owners and their Master Cheesemakers

Kymenlaakso, the area in Finland to which the Stauffer brothers came and where they lived and worked, in some respects didn't differ much from Simmental. We do know that, although they were used to snow and ice, they found the cold in the depth of winter unbearably harsh. There were no mountains here, but nor were there in Simmental low down in the valley on misty days, of which there were many. The characteristic ambience in both these regions was of wooded and rocky hill terrain. The expanses of flat fields and meadows in Elimäki must have been a new experience for them, but at the same time full of promise. The general conditions for agriculture were more favourable here than in Switzerland. There was an almost unlimited supply of arable maiden soil for tillage and pasture. There were no great differences in kind or technique for the cultivation of fields. Livestock rearing and dairying suffered from a lack of dynamism, but it was precisely to improve this that they had been brought to Elimäki.

The customs and habits of local people were familiar, as were attitudes to life and the Protestant religion. The standard of culture and life in the rural population didn't differ much from that on the Simmental farms. The political situation was stable. The Grand Duke headed the country and order and peace prevailed – at least for the time being. And for communicating with their employers and landlords they could use their native language.

Having grown up in a community of smallholders where social standing counted for little, they must have found the landownership and social structure in Elimäki strange. But they had neither reason nor time to dwell on problems that were not theirs. Their business was to get the dairy up and running promptly and cheese production under way to their employers' satisfaction.

Their first few years in Finland happened to be a time of disastrous crop failure and famine (1866–68). It is certainly known that their experiences from this period were less than encouraging. On the other hand the years of shortage may have given them an insight into what was inevitably on the horizon and what changes needed to be made in the structure of Finnish agriculture towards one more reliant on dairy stock. In this they would have pondered their own role and their own possibilities within this process of change. These looked convincingly favourable for them settling down with no obstacles of note in their path.

Peter (1843–1909) and his wife Margaretha, born Tanelintytär (1842–1918).

Jakob (1846–1931) and his second wife Alvina, born Lindgren (1863–1902).

For Peter and Jakob a new dimension of comfort was soon attained with their marriages to farmers' daughters from Elimäki, Peter to Margareta the daughter of Taneli in 1866 and Jakob to Anna daughter of Malakia in 1870. Peter was 23 and Jakob 24. Christian married later, in 1880 at the age of 41 to Rudolf Klossner's daughter Rosalie. Then 25 years old, Rosalie, who had been brought to Sippola in Finland as an infant, was at the time of her marriage employed in the dairy on the Kuusisto estate near Turku. Jakob was widowed in 1877 and remarried in 1881. His second wife Alvina Lindgren daughter of Taavi was from Motti in Okeroinen (Hollola).

Christian (1839–1929) and his wife Rosalie, born
Klossner (1855–1928).

The brothers were lucky to start their work in Finland in the service of the active and talented af Forselles family. A great number of the members of this family have distinguished themselves as soldiers, economists or in the fields of science and art. The family owned a number of large estates in Elimäki and their decision to start cheese production had a crucial influence on how the Stauffer brothers' lives unfolded.

The family's wealth and extensive property ownership had been created by the legendary Sissi-Jaakko – the merchant Jakob Forsell (1696–1768), later mayor of Loviisa – who when raised to the nobility took the name af Forselles. After becoming wealthy via his trading, sawmill and provisioning for the army, he had bought a great number of estates in southern Finland. In those days he must have been one of the most prominent land-owners in Finland, the total acreage of his estates might well have been close to 100 000 hectares. As a result of the division of the inheritance after him and his ten children, the landed property was split into five large estates in Elimäki, namely Moisio, Mustila, Myllylä, Peippola and Villikkala. In the 1860s these estates were owned by the grandsons of Jakob af Forselles junior – three brothers and two of their cousins.

Moisio Manor. Photograph: Veikko Kyander 1915. The Finnish Heritage Agency.

Moisio, the first place where Christian and Jakob worked in Finland, was owned by Colonel Teodor Ulrik af Forselles (1827–1896). On inheriting the estate in 1861 he left the army and began to run his large farm (total acreage 6 800 hectares) with enthusiasm. Cheese production was begun immediately in 1862 on the Naaranoja subsidiary farm under master cheesemaker Block from Germany. Cheese making at the main farm was started in 1864 with Christian and his compatriot Tschabald as master cheesemakers. Christian's work in Moisio was interrupted in 1867 with his return to Switzerland but resumed in 1874 until 1880, the year he moved to the Andersberg estate in Mäntsälä as a tenant dairyman.

Theodor Ulrik's younger brothers Fredrik and Oskar owned Villikkala and Myllylä. Fredrik (1829–1911) was an officer on active duty and had inherited the estates in 1861. He had left the management of the estates to Oskar (1838–1872), to whom he sold Myllylä's share of 1500 hectares in 1864. Peter initiated cheesemaking on these estates in 1864 on his arrival in Finland. It's worth noting in what young hands the setting up and production of cheese both here and on the other estates in Elimäki was entrusted. The employer was 26 and his master cheesemaker 21. Six years later Peter left the af Forselleses and moved to the Muhniemi estate owned by the Wrede family in the neighbouring parish of Anjala. From there he went on, via Liikala in Sippola, to the Harju estate in Virolahti, but came back to Myllylä in 1888, this time as estate owner.

Myllylä Manor, the old main building. Photograph: Signe Brander 1910. The Finnish Heritage Agency.

There was not enough spare land in the Elimäki inheritance for Lennart af Forselles, the youngest of the Moisio brothers and a magistrate, so he used the money he had inherited to buy the Toivonoja estate in Nastola in 1865. The following year, as his wife's dowry, he took possession of the valuable Koiskala estate in the same parish. He started cheese production in Toivonoja in the early 1870s.

Mustila was owned by a cousin of the afore-mentioned brothers, General Ernst af Forselles. Also on this estate cheese production was begun in 1864 with Bühler from Simmental as the master cheesemaker.

Peippola Manor, the old main building. Photograph: Signe Brander 1910. The Finnish Heritage Agency.

The main estate Peippola was run by the head of the family, Pehr Emil af Forselles, who had inherited it at the age of 20 in 1860. It comprised 4 600 hectares. Pehr Emil took vigorous measures to modernise cultivation and cattle breeding on his estate, and so started a cheese dairy as soon as he took over. His master cheesemakers were Baumgartner and Gertsch and from 1874 onwards Jakob Stauffer who came over from Moisio. Jakob was loyal to Peippola, first as an employee and later as a lease-holder until 1894, when he moved to his own estate near Kouvola.

The af Forselleses were fated to lose their landed property. In the early 1870s there was a particularly strong and intense boom which led to Lennart and Pehr Emil getting into the sawmill and timber export business. Lennart founded the Vehka mill at Pernaja, Pehr Emil the sawmill at Hämeenkylä. To do this they had to invest a lot of loan capital in the timber stocks which, for Lennart, had to be guaranteed by the other brothers. The premature deaths of both Lennart and Oskar, at a time when business was slack due to a slump in timber prices, led to a catastrophic situation. Teodor Ulrik tried to stabilise things by taking over the business with its liabilities but failed. All the people involved lost their estates, which sold off under a compulsory order.

Duke Friedrich Berg from Livonia bought Moisio and Villikkala in 1880. Peippola was transferred to Pehr Emil's brother-in-law, Colonel Alexander Etholen, in 1893 and Myllylä to Peter Stauffer in 1888. Only Mustila remained in the family's possession. The prices paid for the estates under the compulsory order were: Moisio 675 000 gold marks, Villikkala 209 000, Peippola 800 000 and Myllylä 178 000 without movables. During the years 1874–1914 the Finnish mark was tied to gold. One gold mark was equivalent to one Swiss gold franc.

Despite the change in ownership cheese production continued at Elimäki. Berg himself didn't move to the area but left the management of the Moisio and Villikkala estates to Otto Wrede, a well-known agricultural expert well-versed in cheese production.

The af Forselleses played a significant role in establishing cheese production in this country during the pre-industrial phase. It was thanks to them that this new field of production as launched by von Daehn in Sippola in 1856 gained a firmer foothold and broader scope. It's worth remembering that the cheese dairies starting production in the 1860s had all been established by the af Forselleses. It was only with the dawning of a new decade in 1870 that some other estates started to get into the business, such as Muhniemi in Anjala, Kalho in Hartola, Perheniemi in Iitti, Ilonoja in Jaala, and Sarvilahti and Malmgård in Pernaja.

It would not be wrong to claim that cheese production in this country first saw the light of day in Sippola, but its cradle was Elimäki thanks to the far-sighted activity of the af Forselleses.

The dairy of Myllylä. Photograph probably from the turn of 20th century.

Elimäki retained its position as the central focus of cheese production for a long time, and it was only in the 1880s that the centre of gravity began to shift to neighbouring parishes to the south. Finland's first set of dairy statistics in 1907 make clear that the three leading parishes for cheese production were :

| Pernaja | 151 000 kg |
| --- | --- |
| Lapinjärvi | 127 000 kg |
| Elimäki | 93 000 kg |

The total production in the country as a whole for the said year was 1 366 000 kg. Judging by today's standards a cheese dairy from the 1860s was small and old-fashioned with the cheese being made in the old Swiss mountain fashion. This meant it was normally produced in a 550-litre cauldron over an open fire using a trammel hook. The product was a wheel of up to 50 kg called Swiss cheese, the "little" Emmental. As the annual milk yield from cows was under 1 000 kg and as milk was also needed for local consumption and butter-making, there was only enough milk left over for one wheel a day even on larger estates. Only in Moisio and Peippola might it have been possible to produce more loaves a day in summer. Thus the annual production of the best estate dairies was in the region of 5 000–10 000 kg which, domestic demand being minimal, was sold to Petersburg cheese-dealers at a price of two gold marks (2 gold francs) a loaf. This made annual gross value of the cheese production for an estate dairy of 10 000 to 20 000 gold marks.

The dairy buildings and equipment were modest. The most expensive investment was in building a cheese cellar, which needed to be solidly built of stone and big enough for storing half a year's production, in other words over 100 wheels. Consumers in Petersburg preferred a more mature, stronger-tasting cheese.

There is no need to get into an explanation of all the difficulties involved in the master cheesemaker's work in those days. But let it be said they didn't have an easy time. The cheese-making process, although it can't be regarded as particularly complicated, required a lot of work and above all precision and care in combination with skill and experience. Controlling the quality of the milk to avoid a faulty maturation due to impurities in the milk required a sharp eye. Workshops were damp and smoky. Salting and storage, both of which required professional skill and physical strength, had to be carried out in damp and dark cellars lit only by a taper or lantern.

There is an amusing fragment we can read in the history of Sippola concerning Klossner's work, as told by an eye-witness, that is a comment on the process. "In summer it was a magnificent sight when 150 head of cattle were being moved from one pasture to another. The procession was always accompanied by a cauldron followed by a cart carrying the herdsman's hut and a herd of grunting pigs waiting for the cheese whey." Similar sights surely awaited a traveller on the roads of Elimäki.

In those days the main road from the centre of Elimäki to Peippola and thence to Moisio had a border of birch saplings, and it was here on the 3-kilometre stretch of road that the Swiss master cheesemakers working on the local estates were in the habit of meeting up at the end of a day's work to chat about the latest news on butter and cheese from the St Petersburg stock market. Nothing is left of the birches today other than a few stumps. Likewise the 'post-feudal' community, which Moisio castle at the end of the avenue came to symbolize has also disappeared. Events in Elimäki in the 1870s set in motion a torrent of social changes that consequently offered the Stauffers in Finland a different life course from that which had been envisaged for them at home in Ringoldingen.

# The Path towards Becoming an Independent Farmer and Trader

As outlined above, the Stauffer brothers began cheese-making as experts employed on the af Forselleses' estates, a phase in their lives which lasted ten years or so. They produced cheese and butter on behalf of the estate and at the same time were responsible for cattle breeding and its development in general. Selling and marketing were the concern of the estate owner.

No information exists about the level or structure of their wages, not even whether it was a fixed sum or whether it varied according to the amount of cheese produced. But it can be assumed that the pay was relatively good. Master cheesemakers were valued employees in the running of estates. It was by means of their work that in the 1860s, when frosts several times destroyed the crops and timber had little market value, that the estates got almost their entire income. Even though estates subsisted pretty much on a barter economy, solid cash was also needed. Life in St Petersburg was expensive. Many of the af Forselleses were military men, lived in Russia, and needed financial backing from their estates. Siblings' share of the inheritance, the interest on debts, the mechanisation of agriculture, foreign travel and children's studies all required hard cash. In the early 1870s good harvests together with a sharp rise in the price of timber led to a strengthening of the cash flow but at the same time were behind some of the family members' more reckless schemes, which as we have seen led to financial ruin.

The dairy of Peippola. At the gable end of the building an apartment was reserved for the leaseholder Jakob's family. Photograph probably at the end of the 19<sup>th</sup> century.

The closing years of the 1870s meant far-reaching changes in the lives of the Stauffer brothers too. This was the period in which they managed to rise above being paid employees and become dairy lease-holders. One source links this new-found independence to the Russo-Turkish war of 1877–78, when "the sale of cheese was at an almost complete standstill and cheese cellars full, the whole cheese-making industry was threatened with ruin". These were also the years which saw a general economic slump. At the time Christian and Jakob were still in the af Forselleses' employ, while Peter was at the Liikala estate owned by Countess Helena van Suchtelen in Sippola. The reasons for dairy production on estates changing onto a leasehold basis can be found in their ownership structure. A great number of owners lived elsewhere as state officials, military men, heirs, widows and bankruptcy receivers, and therefore seldom lived permanently on their estates and were seldom in touch with their business activities. Under these circumstances the change was therefore logical since it brought efficiencies and progress to the business. Lease-holding gradually won the support of estate owners and within a period of less than 30 years had become the standard means of collaboration between estates and master cheesemakers. Many dairy co-operatives, before moving to cheese production on their own account, adopted the practice.

Leasing used to be based on an agreement by which an estate or co-operative society leased its dairy plus equipment to a cheesemaker for a fixed period of time, and the lessee undertook to pay a fixed price for the milk supplied. The price paid to landlords in the 1880s and later was about 10 pennis per litre. This was slightly higher than the price the landlords would have got by producing butter. At the same time it was a bit lower than the retail price of milk to consumers in population centres. Milk producers made it a habit to auction lease-holdings of their dairies, which must have put a severe strain on solidarity among the Swiss.

In 1880 Christian left Elimäki to go to Mäntsälä where he worked as a lease-holder of the Andersberg dairy owned by von Qvanten family. After Liikala was taken over by the State, Peter in 1883 leased the Harju estate dairy in Virojoki owned by A. von Knorring. A couple of years later this estate was also transferred to the State as the site for an agricultural school and so Peter became a lease-holder of the State. A lease-holding contract exists from this period, one of the few written documents in which the dairy lessee's rights and obligations are made explicit. Here it is in its entirety :

1. Stauffer undertakes to buy the whole milk production from Harju and Riko and to pay 9.7 pennis pr kilo for it.
2. Stauffer is in charge of feeding the cattle in the Harju cow-shed under the supervision of the headman with regard to the amount of fodder and other instructions, and in this he will be assisted by 4 milkmaids and in winter one farmhand, all of whom will receive their wages from the estate.
3. Every year Stauffer must raise 10–15 calves and give them milk according to instructions.
4. He will have the use of the Harju dairy together with all the firewood and supply of ice therein needed, and for his accommodation 2 rooms and kitchen belonging to the dairy. In addition a small potato plot will be available for his use.
5. Stauffer can use all equipment belonging to the dairy against an annual payment that is 3% of its purchase price, and at the end of the lease period he must leave everything in a condition fit for use.
6. Stauffer can use the estate piggery and receive the necessary litter for the pigs.
7. Stauffer will have 50 man-work days a year for transporting butter and cheese.

This agreement expired on November 1st, 1892.

The lease contract surprisingly makes no mention of the length of the payment period for the milk and so cannot enlighten us on the interesting question of how Peter or the other cheese producers managed to finance their business in the early phase of the lease-holding. It is unlikely that they would have managed to save more than a couple of thousand gold marks from their salaries while at the same time a quite considerable sum of money would have been tied up in storing the cheese for six months. The brothers are not known to have received any financial assistance from home in Switzerland, nor would bank credit have been available to them at this stage. What is likely is that the estates and other milk producers granted favourable terms of payment and the Saint Petersburg cheese merchants advance payments, allowing them to pay off the deficits of the first few years.

Becoming independent dairy lease-holders meant the beginning of a new period for the brothers involving essentially a wider liberty of action. Now they had the possibility to organise their business activities however they themselves saw fit. They had a right to buy extra milk from outside the estate, to hire assistants, to found and run subsidiaries (Christian the Kullo dairy in Porvoo parish and Peter Ilonoja in Jaala). They were able to make adjustments to the production lines of cheese, butter and pork the better to match economic trends and to choose the best moment for selling their products. This gave them added incentive to follow the latest developments in their field and to modernise.

This was a period when market prices favoured cheese production. Cheese and butter were priced more or less the same, 2 gold marks a kilo. Bearing in mind that 12 kilos of milk were needed for one kilo of cheese but 30 kilos for butter, there was therefore a decided price advantage in favour of cheese production. The purchase price of the milk required to produce one kilo of cheese was 1.20 gold marks. Thus the master cheesemaker made a net income of about 80 pennis per kilo of cheese in return for his own expertise and as profit, always assuming that the by-products of the process, namely butter and pork, were enough to cover the assistants' pay and other expenses. A medium-sized dairy with annual output of 10 000 kilos yielded its successful entrepreneur about 8 000 gold marks per annum of net income. In those days this was the annual salary of a fairly senior civil servant. In this connection it is worth drawing attention to the word "successful", since success was by no means a foregone conclusion in the field. Nothing more complicated than a detrimental strain of bacteria in the milk producer's herd could lead to a sub-standard product and so to economic ruin for the master cheesemaker.

The first few years of the brothers' lease-holding coincided with a time when agriculture in this country was experiencing a strong general revival and production was branching into new directions. There was a tendency for agricultural production to focus more on animal husbandry than on growing food grain as previously. The spirit of the times was captured in the declaration that "Hunger will not come to an end before rye stacks disappear from the fields". There was a drive to intensify cattle and dairy farming to such an extent that exports of dairy products would compensate for imports of food grain. Improved pedigrees, and intensifying cultivation of fodder and meadowland, helped bring about the desired result. At the same time as the number of cows was growing, the average annual milk yield per cow also increased from barely 900 kilos in the 1870s to 1 100 kilos at the end of the century. It has been estimated that total milk production for the period 1880 to 1909 more than doubled.

In 1909 59% of milk production was used for butter, 2% for cheese and 38% for consumption. That year 12 million kilos of dairy butter were produced, 1.5 million kilos of cheese and 35 million kilos of homemade butter, quantities which point to the difficulty in a sparsely-populated country with limited means of transport of getting the milk to a centralised refinery.

The increase in the quantity of milk produced and strong support from the State brought about the heated expansion in dairy activity during the 1880s, when plenty of new dairies were established. It was calculated in 1891 that there were 859 of them. Although dairying was focused mainly on production of butter, it was natural that the general upswing was also reflected strongly in cheese production. The number of dairies producing cheese grew from 20 in the 1870s to nearly one hundred at the turn of the century.

Increasing quantities of milk from individual dairies made it possible to use larger vats, first 850 litres and then 1050 litres, and start producing full-size Emmental wheels of 80–90 kilos. Open fireplaces and trammel hooks were replaced by permanent brick-built vats with their own chimneys and so-called "fire trolleys" that allowed much easier regulation of the heat. In the 1890s larger dairies introduced steam heating, separators and other technical improvements, while the work areas began to be more solidly built in a more up-to-date way. The pre-industrial phase in cheese production was coming to an end.

Products were sold in Saint Petersburg and elsewhere in Russia at a relatively competitive price due to them being exempt from the 100% customs surcharge. The worst pressure on prices came from cheese dairies in the Baltic provinces.

A meeting at the *Kouvolan hotelli*. Peter in the middle, Jakob on the right, third person unidentified. Photograph: G.H. Andersson probably from the turn of the 20th century.

Under these favourable conditions the Stauffer brothers as lease-holders of major estate dairies – Christian in Andersberg, Peter in Harju and Jakob in Peippola – could relatively easily achieve economic stability. In addition to their 25 years of experience, they were starting to have sufficient material resources to realise their hopes of breaking free from their lease liabilities and also to reduce their dependence on compulsory milk purchases. Owning the dairy themselves and having the milk production in their own hands would help guarantee continuity under changing external conditions and would give them more latitude than before to develop the production and business. In those days the most pressing problem in cheese production was how to obtain sufficient quantities of milk. Productivity was hampered by scarcity and large seasonal fluctuations. In summer milk was in abundance and so it was necessary to make so-called "night cheese", but in winter there wasn't enough milk to make even one full-size wheel. The prevailing situation is illustrated by the notice of lease-hold auction for the Liljendahl co-op dairy in 1880. This co-operative society situated in the heartlands of such a large area of cultivation could even then guarantee the tenant a minimum quantity of milk per day of only 300 litres. This amount was far from sufficient for a cheesemaker.

All three brothers acquired citizenship of their new homeland in the same year, 1888. This was necessary for purchasing landed property, which they then proceeded to do. Christian bought Miettilä in Rautu, Peter Myllylä in Elimäki and Jakob Puosila near Kouvola.

At the time the brothers were approaching 50 years of age, which meant they still had many productive years ahead of them as independent landowners and dairymen before retiring to enjoy their twilight years.

Owning their own farms and dairies reinforced their economic and social position, but Peter was the only brother to achieve the goal of freeing himself of the compulsory purchase of milk for his cheesemaking. By overhauling and expanding cultivation at Myllylä and then taking a lease-hold on the Anjala estate owned by Prince Menšikov he was assured of 200–300 kilos of cheese a day from his own cattle's milk. Christian and Jakob also significantly expanded their cultivation and cattle-breeding at Miettilä and Puosila, but the milk yield there was not sufficient for fully efficient cheese-making. It proved difficult to obtain the required quantities of extra milk from neighbouring farms because in Rautu this tended to be bought up for St Petersburg, and Kouvola as an emergent residential area needed it for consumption. Christian resolved the problem by taking a lease on the Ivaska dairy in neighbouring Räisälä while Jakob quit cheese-making soon after moving to Puosila in 1895 and started selling milk for consumption.

The first of the brothers to die was Peter in 1909 at the age of 66, then Christian in 1929 at 90 and Jakob two years later at 85. Many of their sons continued in their father's profession.

The lively resurgence of the dairy business in the 1880s was accompanied by a corresponding surge in the influx of Swiss dairymen to Finland. About one hundred new cheesemakers arrived in the country during the period 1880–1900. Of these, some found a position as leaseholders for estate or co-operative dairies, others as employees and assistants in dairies owned by an older generation of master cheesemakers.

Anna (1834–1911).

Annas husband
Friedrich Wiedmer (1834–
1908)

It is not surprising that amongst these should be found three of the Stauffers' brothers-in-law, namely Anna's, Verena's and Susanna's husbands. It was quite natural for the relatives in Switzerland to follow the progress of the brothers' affairs with interest. Their communications from Finland gradually began to take on a more and more encouraging tone as first-hand information on favourable conditions and good earning possibilities gradually kindled interest within the sisters' families.

Friedrich Wiedmer resigned his post as a schoolteacher, completed a course of studies in professional cheese-making, and left for Finland with Anna and their six children in 1885. Friedrich and Anna were already in their 50s and their eldest sons almost 20. The family settled down in Lapinjärvi, where Friedrich worked as a lease-holder in various estate dairies until his death in 1908. All three sons and sons-in-law became master cheesemakers in eastern Uusimaa. One of these sons was the first to start making cheese in Savo in 1905. Anna died three years after her husband at the age of 79.

Verena (1845–1931) and her husband
Benedickt Weibel  (1852–1927).

In 1885 Benedickt and Verena Weibel also set out for Finland with their 3-year old daughter. At first the family settled at brother Jakob's in Peippola but moved to Heinjoki the following year, where Benedickt had managed to lease the dairy business at Ristseppälä estate owned by

A. Grotenfelt. Here Benedickt built a dairy on the estate and started cheese production. The estate comprised 10 000 hectares and it was said that in its fields "hay was growing so thick that a cuckoo could sit on the stems and sing". Four years later in 1890 ownership of the estate was transferred to the State for 600 000 gold marks and split up between tenant farmers. 164 independent farms were created. In addition to his cheese production Benedickt practised farming and a retail business. The dairy began to suffer from a shortage of milk as more and more of the area's production made its way to Viipuri (Vyborg) and St Petersburg for consumption, and so cheese production at Ristseppälä finally came to an end in the early 1920s. Benedickt died in 1927 and Verena four years later at the age of 86.

Susanna (1848–1930) and her husband Christian Eggen (1850–1922).

Christian and Susanna Eggen arrived in Finland in 1896 with three sons and two daughters, leaving the eldest son in Switzerland. Christian had sold his family farm in Därsteten and shortly after his arrival took a lease-hold on the Latokartano estate dairy in Lapinjärvi, a large farm owned by the State. After running the farm with its dairy and cattle for two years with his sons' help, Christian in 1898 returned to Switzerland with his wife and daughters. The Latokartano lease was then taken over by one of his sons. The younger sons found employment as dairy assistants with relatives and a couple of years later started operating as independent lease-holders. The Eggens' daughters married master cheesemakers who had emigrated to Finland. In the early 1900s interest in cheese production had started to spread to the estates and cooperatives in the western parts of the country. It was here that many of the Eggens and their brothers-in-law found their calling. After their return to Switzerland Christian and Susanna settled down on a small farm in Boltingen. Susanna was widowed in 1922 and spent the remaining years of her life with her children, partly in Finland and partly in Switzerland. She died in 1930 at the age of 82.

The numerous brothers and brothers-in-law of the Wiedmers and the Eggens formed a considerable contingent of a dozen or so men in the band of professional cheesemakers in this country, as did a good number of their sons.

Thus it was the remarkable destiny of a Simmental couple, Samuel and Katharina Stauffer, to be in the unprecedented position where their descendants who had settled in Finland were responsible at its peak for a quarter of this country's cheese production at the beginning of the 20th century. Annual output at that time was slightly more than one million kilos. The equivalent figure nowadays is approaching one hundred million kilos. This is more than the production of butter and not much less than production in Switzerland, which in 1980 totalled 124 million kilos. About half of Finland's production is sold abroad and the income from it is not insignificant in the national economy.

It has taken one hundred years to progress from the original estate-dairy idyll to the concentrated production of today's giant dairies. The structure of the industry and the production techniques have undergone a thorough upheaval. As one example, it became evident in the early 1950s that estate and lease-hold dairies were too small to be efficient and profitable. The master cheesemakers of old have also disappeared in the light of progress and been superseded by micro-biologists and industrial computer technology experts.

The changing structure of this country's economic activity has been strongly reflected in the Stauffer family's professional profile. Whereas with a few exceptions the second generation of the family found their life's work in dairy farming and agriculture, precious few of the third generation born in the early 20th century followed in their fathers' footsteps professionally speaking. As far as is known only one family member is working in dairy production and no more than a few as farmers.

At the Emmental cheese presses Jakob's son Jaakko Valdemar Stauffer (1890–1959). Photograph from the early 1910s.